To:

From:

FELIZ NAVIDAD
NOLLAIG SHONA DHUIT
MERRY
CHRISTMAS
Buon Natale
JOYEUX NOËL
FRÖHLICHE
WEIHNACHTEN

WINTER IS THE TIME
FOR **COMFORT**,
FOR **GOOD FOOD** AND
WARMTH, FOR THE
TOUCH OF A FRIENDLY
HAND AND FOR A
TALK BESIDE THE FIRE:
IT IS THE TIME
FOR **HOME**.

—*Edith Sitwell*

SNOW
FLURRIES
BEGAN TO FALL
AND THEY *swirled*
AROUND PEOPLE'S LEGS
LIKE HOUSE CATS. IT WAS
magical, THIS SNOW
GLOBE WORLD.
—Sarah Addison
Allen

JUST REMEMBER,
THE TRUE SPIRIT
OF CHRISTMAS LIES IN
YOUR HEART.

—The Polar Express

HAPPY CHRISTMAS TO ALL, AND TO ALL A GOOD-NIGHT.

—Clement C. Moore

ON A COLD, SNOWY NIGHT, EVERYONE AND EVERYTHING SHOULD BE WELCOMED SOMEWHERE.

—Lemony Snicket

RING OUT,
WILD BELLS,
TO THE
WILD SKY,
THE FLYING
CLOUD, THE
**FROSTY
LIGHT.**

*—Alfred, Lord
Tennyson*

ON CHRISTMAS
DAY, WE WILL
SHUT OUT FROM
OUR FIRESIDE,
NOTHING.
—*Charles Dickens,*
WHAT CHRISTMAS
IS AS WE GROW OLDER

IT IS A SEASON THAT
KNOWS WHAT A
GOOD GIFT IS,
ONE THAT KEEPS
ON GIVING,
ECHOING DOWN
THE HARD WALLS
TIME MAKES.

—*Justin Isherwood*

SOMETHING
ABOUT AN
OLD-FASHIONED
CHRISTMAS IS HARD
TO FORGET.

—Hugh Downs

CHRISTMAS COMES DURING A SEASON WHEN THE EARTH IS IN ITS **DARKEST TIME.** IT'S A HOLIDAY FOR THE FAMILY AND FOR **EVERYONE.**

—*Melissa Etheridge*

THE **ORNAMENT**
OF A HOUSE IS THE
FRIENDS WHO
FREQUENT IT.

—*Ralph Waldo Emerson*

HOMEMADE
COOKIES ARE ONE OF
THE BEST PARTS
OF CHRISTMAS.

—Dean Koontz

WHAT HAPPENS AT THE CHRISTMAS PARTY STAYS AT THE CHRISTMAS PARTY.

THERE'S SOMETHING
ABOUT A
CHRISTMAS
SWEATER
THAT WILL ALWAYS
MAKE ME LAUGH.

—Kristen Wiig

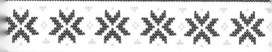

HAVE YOURSELF A MERRY LITTLE CHRISTMAS.

—Hugh Martin

...FRESHLY CUT
CHRISTMAS TREES
SMELLING OF *stars* AND
snow AND PINE RESIN—
INHALE DEEPLY AND
FILL YOUR SOUL WITH
WINTRY NIGHT.

—*John Geddes*

YOU MIGHT AS WELL
DO YOUR CHRISTMAS
HINTING
EARLY.

—Author Unknown

CHRISTMAS RENEWS
OUR YOUTH BY
STIRRING OUR
WONDER. THE
CAPACITY FOR WONDER
HAS BEEN CALLED OUR
MOST PREGNANT
HUMAN FACULTY,
FOR IN IT ARE BORN
OUR ART, OUR SCIENCE,
OUR RELIGION.

—*Ralph Sockman*

A **CHRISTMAS CANDLE** IS A LOVELY THING; IT MAKES NO NOISE AT ALL BUT *softly* GIVES ITSELF **AWAY**

—*Eva K. Logue*

A BIG ORANGE
AND SOME FRESH
PINE BOUGHS AND
"Silent Night" ARE ALL
I NEED, AND *cookies*,
OF *course.*

—*Garrison Keillor*

UP ON THE HOUSETOP

REINDEER PAUSE,

OUT JUMPS GOOD OLD

SANTA CLAUS.

—*Benjamin Hanby*

IT IS . . .
THE SEASON FOR
kindling NOT
MERELY THE FIRE OF
HOSPITALITY IN THE
HALL, BUT THE GENIAL
FLAME OF CHARITY
IN THE HEART.

—*Washington Irving*

CHRISTMAS WAS
ON ITS WAY.
LOVELY, GLORIOUS,
BEAUTIFUL
CHRISTMAS, UPON
WHICH THE ENTIRE

kid year

REVOLVED.

—Jean Shepherd,
A CHRISTMAS STORY

OUR **HEARTS**
GROW TENDER WITH
CHILDHOOD
MEMORIES AND
LOVE OF KINDRED,
AND WE ARE BETTER
THROUGHOUT THE YEAR
FOR HAVING, IN SPIRIT,
BECOME A **CHILD**
AGAIN AT
CHRISTMAS-TIME.

—Laura Ingalls Wilder

CHRISTMAS EVE
WAS A NIGHT OF *song*
THAT WRAPPED
ITSELF ABOUT YOU
LIKE A *shawl*.
—*Bess Streeter Aldrich*

YOU KNOW
YOU'RE
grown up WHEN
NONE OF THE
THINGS YOU
REALLY WANT
FOR CHRISTMAS
COST MONEY.

STOP AND SMELL THE GINGERBREAD.

Ho ho ho

EVERY TIME
A BELL RINGS,
AN ANGEL GETS
HIS WINGS.
—*Zuzu*,
IT'S A WONDERFUL LIFE

I WILL *honour*
CHRISTMAS IN
MY *heart*, AND
TRY TO KEEP IT
all the year.

—*Charles Dickens*,
A CHRISTMAS CAROL

DEEP IN OUR HEARTS,
WE SECRETLY
HOPE THAT . . .
CHRISTMAS WILL
RENDER US
VULNERABLE
ENOUGH TO
EXPERIENCE
ANTICIPATION,
BELIEF AND
INNOCENCE.

—David Caldwell

EVERY DECORATION
AND ORNAMENT
HAS A **STORY.**
. . . EVERY YEAR,
AS WE GO ABOUT
MAKING THE HOUSE
LOOK AS **MAGICAL**
AS WE CAN, WE
RECONNECT
TO OUR **PAST.**

—Mary Engelbreit

LET IT SNOW.

TOO MUCH OF A GOOD THING CAN BE WONDERFUL.

—Mae West

SLEEP IN
HEAVENLY
PEACE.

—Joseph Mohr,
SILENT NIGHT

ONE OF THE MOST
GLORIOUS
MESSES IN THE
WORLD IS THE **MESS**
CREATED IN THE
LIVING ROOM ON
CHRISTMAS DAY.
DON'T CLEAN IT UP
TOO **QUICKLY.**

—Andy Rooney

GOOD *times*,
GOOD *friends*,
GOOD *cheer*.

IT IS THE PERSONAL
THOUGHTFULNESS,
THE WARM HUMAN
AWARENESS, THE
REACHING OUT OF THE
SELF TO ONE'S FELLOW
MAN THAT MAKES
GIVING WORTHY
OF THE CHRISTMAS
SPIRIT.

—Isabel Currier

I HEARD THE BELLS
ON *Christmas Day*
THEIR OLD,
FAMILIAR CAROLS *play*,
AND WILD AND SWEET
THE WORDS REPEAT
OF *peace on earth*,
GOOD-WILL TO MEN!

*—Henry Wadsworth
Longfellow*

KEEP CALM

AND

BE MERRY.

YES, *Virginia*,
THERE **IS**
A **SANTA**
CLAUS.

—*Francis Pharcellus*
Church

I LIKE TO TAKE
MY CHRISTMAS
A *little* AT A TIME,
ALL **THROUGH**
THE YEAR.

—David Grayson

MAYBE *Christmas*,
HE THOUGHT,
DOESN'T COME
FROM A STORE.
MAYBE *Christmas*,
PERHAPS, MEANS
A LITTLE BIT
MORE.

—*Dr. Seuss*,
THE GRINCH WHO
STOLE CHRISTMAS

THE PERFECT

CHRISTMAS TREE?

All CHRISTMAS

TREES ARE

PERFECT!

—*Charles N. Barnard*

IT'S CHRISTMAS DAY! I HAVEN'T MISSED IT.

—Scrooge,

IN **A CHRISTMAS CAROL**
BY CHARLES DICKENS

CHRISTMAS WAVES A
MAGIC WAND
OVER THIS WORLD,
AND **BEHOLD**,
EVERYTHING IS
softer AND MORE
beautiful.
—Norman Vincent Peale

THE MOON IS HID;
THE NIGHT
IS STILL;
THE CHRISTMAS
BELLS FROM
HILL TO HILL
ANSWER EACH OTHER
IN THE MIST.

—*Alfred, Lord Tennyson*

REMEMBRANCE,
LIKE A CANDLE,
burns brightest AT
CHRISTMASTIME.

—*Charles Dickens*

WISHING YOU *warmth* AND

festive cheer,

AND HAPPINESS TO

LAST THROUGH THE

WHOLE *new year.*

I WAS NEVER
ALONE AT ALL.
THAT, OF COURSE,
WAS THE
MESSAGE
OF CHRISTMAS.
WE ARE
never alone.

—Taylor Caldwell

WHAT IS *Christmas*? IT IS TENDERNESS FOR THE **PAST**, COURAGE FOR THE **PRESENT**, HOPE FOR THE **FUTURE**.

—*Agnes M. Pahro*

AT CHRISTMAS,
ALL ROADS LEAD
home.

—*Marjorie Holmes*

HEAR THE SLEDGES
WITH THE BELLS—
SILVER BELLS!
WHAT A WORLD OF
merriment
THEIR MELODY
FORETELLS!

—*Edgar Allan Poe*

Get your jingle on.

AS A BOY, I KNEW
WITH CERTAINTY
THAT REINDEER
could fly.
—*Robert Sullivan*

CALL A **TRUCE**, THEN,
TO OUR LABORS—*let us*
feast WITH FRIENDS
AND **NEIGHBORS**.
—*Rudyard Kipling*

Joy to the world!

—Isaac Watts,
CHRISTMAS CAROL

IN THE COUNTRY,
IT IS SO QUIET
THAT YOU CAN
ALMOST HEAR
the chime OF EACH
SNOWFLAKE AS IT
GENTLY FALLS.

—*Amy Rost-Holtz*

EGGBEATERS WHIRL,
spoons spin round
IN BOWLS OF BUTTER
AND **SUGAR,** *vanilla*
SWEETENS THE AIR . . .

—*Truman Capote,*
A CHRISTMAS MEMORY

THE DARK IS NOISY
AND BRIGHT WITH
LATE-NIGHT ARRIVALS—
doors thrown open,
RUNNING SHADOWS
ON SNOW, OPEN ARMS,
KISSES, VOICES
AND LAUGHTER.
—Elizabeth Bowen,
HOME FOR CHRISTMAS

Merry Christmas, Sugar Plum

THE TALL TREES
TURNED INTO
ARBRES DE
NOËL, TWINKLING
WITH THOUSANDS OF
LITTLE LIGHTS
THE COLOR OF
CHAMPAGNE.

—M. F. K. Fisher

CHRISTMAS DAY

IN THE COMPANY
OF CHILDREN IS ONE
OF THE FEW
OCCASIONS ON WHICH
MEN BECOME
ENTIRELY ALIVE.

—Robert Lynd

'TIS THE SEASON

to be jolly.

FA LA LA LA LA
LA LA LA LA . . .

—*Thomas Oliphant,*
DECK THE HALLS

Dear Santa,
I can explain . . .

CHRISTMAS ISN'T
JUST A DAY,
IT'S A FRAME
OF MIND.
—*Kris Kringle,*
MIRACLE ON 34TH STREET

life is filled with light and love, promise and possibility. So when the nights grow longer and the trees twinkle with strings of lights, make space for the peace and wonder of Yuletide. Go for a stroll to take it all in, curl up with a cup of cocoa, and—above all—bask in the glow of your beloved friends and family, who add more magic to the season than any garlands, gifts, or songs.

Have yourself a merry little Christmas and a Happy New Year!

INTRODUCTION

THE TRUE CHRISTMAS BATHES EVERY LITTLE THING IN LIGHT.

–*Garrison Keillor*

'Tis the season to be jolly, so get your jingle on! But even as you jump into the holiday fray—shopping, sending cards, decking the halls, and decorating cookies— don't forget to stop and smell the gingerbread. Because this is also a time to remember that

KEEP CALM AND BE MERRY

DEAR SANTA

HOLIDAY HUGS

SUGAR PLUMS

CHRISTMAS

Fa la la la la la la la la la . . .

CANDLELIGHT

GET YOUR JINGLE ON

GOOD TIMES

HOMEMADE COOKIES

To all the friends and family
who keep our winters warm and bright

Designed by Tesslyn Pandarakalam
Illustrations from Shutterstock.com

Visit us at www.peterpauper.com

CHRISTMAS

*Written and compiled
by Talia Levy
and Suzanne Schwalb*

PETER PAUPER PRESS, INC.
White Plains, New York